THE EUPHONIES

(The Poetic Voice Of God)

AMARA Ifeakor -Ezenwa

Liberation Publishers
The publishing body of The Liberation Court International Gospel Centre
9 rue Jack Kerouac 35700 Rennes, France.

EUPHONIES (The Poetic Voice Of God)

ISBN 978-2-487298-13-2

APPRECIATION

I AM ONLY A clay in Your pottery stand and a ready pen in Your genius hand.

Can a finished vessel boast of its finesse? And can a pen boast of its mastery? So can no one take the glory for this work, but You !

PRELUDE

You speak to men in divers means
   Through trance and dreams and other ways
   You pick each man and choose the means
   That will best appeal to his very being
   So that Your will and Your thought may be
   truly clear to all human beings
   So this time You have chosen
   To let me hear Your poetic tone

INTRODUCTION

THE EUPHONIES IS A collection of poems that are written at different times and occasions. These poems comprise expressions of deep, personal struggles, perceptions, questions, disappointments, and God's comforting words and miraculous interventions at those times.

The aim of this work of art is to uncover the hope that is found in the recognition that God is with us, a very present Help in trouble. He also speaks to His children poetically.

I wish you a happy read!

CONTENTS

1

I'VE GONE NOWHERE

Is it down the abysmal end of the valley
  Where no mortal can reach?
  Or up above the mountain summit
  Where no eagle ever perched?
  Beyond the horizon of thoughts
  Eyes bewildered in search of him
  Where has he gone?

  The fragrance of roses seem so bare
  The radiance of sun seems so queer
  The road looks longer
  The paths feel rougher
  The burden gets heavier
  Yet the stream seems drier
  Where has he gone ?

Our tongues parch for lack of water
Our hearts fail for want untold
We have reached the crossroad
We have been stretched beyond limit
The whole structure is torn apart
The remedy is still unknown
Where has he gone ?

We do not know why it's this tough
We cannot tell why it's so rough
Neither do we know the next turn
For the tide is ever high
Will our boat make it to the shore?
Beyond the reach of the angry storm
Where has he gone?

« Here am I, I've gone nowhere »
In good and in bad, am here to stay
In the midst of the waves and the storms
My presence is there to soothe the pains
I am not hidden in a place so far
I only reside within your heart
I am here to hold your hand!

2

WHERE ARE YOU GOING ?

WHERE ARE YOU GOING ?
  Please go back to wherever
  Or whichever place you desire
  But not here anymore
  For there's no more space
  Not even a foot
  Your remains are all thrown out
  Far faraway
  Out of eyesight
  Out of earshot

  Can we forget in a hurry?
  The long nights of agony
  We shiver to remember
  The pains unimaginable
  The sorrows unbearable

The grinning of teeth
The bouts of trauma
All these and even more
Symbolize your first visit

So where again are you going?
What again are you doing ?
Lurking around the corner
Looking for a space to enter
To regain possession?
To continue your devastation?
Of utter suppression
Of total frustration
Of absolute humiliation

You better keep off OSTEOARTHRITIS
The same Power that put you to rout
The very first time you struck
He neither sleeps nor slumbers
Jesus Christ the healer
He is still the one in charge
Of this house
Of this temple
Of this body

1

---

1. Written as a face off against the reprisal of Osteoarthritis

3

FORTY LONG DAYS AND FORTY LONG NIGHTS

He stepped into the wilderness
He was all by himself
Amidst snakes and scorpions
To be tempted
To be tried
To be provoked
To be ridiculed
He was all by himself
Forty long days
Forty long nights

He stepped into the wilderness
He was all by himself
Burdened by his earthly mission
Of seeking the lost

Of raising the dead
Of healing the sick
Of sacrificing Himself
He was all by himself
Forty long days
Forty long nights

Then came the tempter
Mocking and sneering
"He says he's God
Can he make stone bread?
Can he bow for a glory?
Can he take a suicidal leap?"
But He endured all the heck
And would not give a break
Forty long days
Forty long nights

From the wilderness He hit the road
His messages brought full salvation
The miracles were beyond comprehension
Through the cross we gained redemption
He went to the grave to complete the rounds
Bringing freedom from death and hades
Now we know it's worth the stress
The forty long days
The forty long nights

4

HOPE RETRIEVED

HE IS SITTING BOUND in their jail
   He used to be their jailer
   Now a captive in their hold
   Caged and chained hands and feet
   Hair shaven and clothes stripped
   The hand work of Delilah

   Wasn't he the captor
   How has he become the captive?
   Wasn't he the conqueror
   How has he become the conquered?
   Looking haggard and tired
   The hand work of Delilah

   His eyes and hair have gone
   The very symbol of his strength

The very relics of his Nazarene birth
Misused and abused by his excesses
Gambled away in the atmosphere of lust
The hand work of Delilah

Tonight he would make them sport
The same people he was born to subdue
The whole people would all converge
To see this object of ridicule
What a humiliating way to die
A prey in the camp of his enemies
Taking orders and obeying orders
Without deliverer, without hope

"Wait! what on earth is he saying
What on earth is he thinking ?
What on earth is he doing ?
Why is he feeling the pillars?
Let's continue our merrymaking
All night long without ending
For he is without deliverer,
He's without hope"

'Help me this once' he was praying
His Deliverer heard his pleading
Then his hair started growing
And then he started pushing
Then the walls started cracking
The pillars started shaking

The congregation started trembling
And the building came crashing

The lesson we are learning
Is that God is never failing
Even when chances are gloomy
Our Deliverer is ever handy

5

DID PILATE KNOW ?

I WAITED TILL THE first day of the week
    But couldn't wait for the first ray of the sun
    To catch the glimpse of His corpse
    A body mutilated by soldiers and haters
    Lying cold inside a tomb
    Finished.
    Forsaken.
    Forgotten.

Did Pilate know
how much He forgave me?
Did the mob know
how much He meant to me?
The tears turned pool?
The hair turned towel?
And the Alabaster pot?

All these in one spot

My heart cut when I bent over
I saw some linens
but not my Lord
"Where did they keep Him?"
"Mary!" He tenderly called
"I am no longer in the grave
I have now risen to reign"

So I leaped for joy untold
For my Savior is now alive
He's defeated death and grave
And restored man back to God
So I run with the good news
Not just for Peter
But also for you

6

TAKE SOME EXTRAS

THE WISE CAME WITH their extras
  For just enough isn't usually enough
  It is a proven fact of life
  The night will sometimes seem longer
  The light may occasionally flicker
  Men's hearts may begin to wander
  And their hope will begin to stagger
  'Cause the groom may somehow linger

  The clarion call finally came
  "The groom is here! the groom is here!"
  The dead night suddenly came alive
  Then the hastening, then the scampering
  Up! the wise jumped and lit their lamps
  Also the fools but in search of oil
  'T was just then the door got closed

Despite the pleading, the bolt was sealed

So here's the wisdom in it all
Never you depend on just enough
Never you forget some 'extras' of faith
For when there are delays on your path
The only force beneath your wings
Will be the extras in your tank of faith

7

SIMPLICITY

I LOVE THE LIFE you define
I love the picture you paint
I love the character you display
I love the dress you wear
I love the words you choose

You speak with the clearest tones
You teach with the finest sense
You do the kindest things
You portray the finest soul
You twinned with humility

You were demonstrated
when He up got from the meal
removed His outer garment
wrapped the towel round His waist

and stooped to wash their feet

For stooping is what is required
to wash not to be washed
Task reserved for the basest
though He's the greatest
He came to serve and not to be served

One by one they took their turn
The betrayers
The doubters
The high minded
And their likes
One by one they took their turn

As He washed He dried
And as He dried He taught
"You have no part in me
except you're washed"
Thus they would learn
that to serve is to lead
And to lead is to serve
The all-time lesson
taught in simplicity

8

Victory At Last

WE ALL WATCHED FROM afar
He was pushed.
Dragged.
Ruffled.
Manhandled.
What happened to those hands?
Weren't they the same hands
That raised Lazarus and others?
Didn't those hands calm the storm?
"Why were they so stiff before the mob?"
Confused beyond words
We kept watching
We held our breath as Pilate lifted the gavel
Death by crucifixion was the verdict

We all watched from afar
He was mocked.
Flogged.
Killed.
What happened to those feet?
They went dead and cold
Who could have told
They would end like this?
Heads bent in dejection
We stole away from the scene
The sun had suddenly hidden her face
Darkness had suddenly engulfed us
Jerusalem had been bereaved of life
She'd been stripped off her dignity

Sleep's been scarce since Friday
It's still very early this morning
Voices were heard afar
Whether it's for joy or sorrow
We could not tell
They kept coming closer
The knock was getting louder
The push on the door was harder
The door knob turning faster
Surely they were coming for us
But who are they?
What on earth do they want?
Haven't they killed our Lord?
Do they want us too?

Eyes weakened by inconsolable tears
Faces paled by agony and fear
We were expecting the worse
But what can be worse
Than the gruesome murder of our Hope?
So we gazed as Peter got the door
Mary and her friends barged in
"He's risen! Our Lord is risen
The grave is empty
Death is swallowed in victory
The sun of righteousness reigns"
With heads now raised in pride
And hearts filled with praise
We celebrate our risen Lord
Who has triumphed over sin and death

9

MEET MY FAMILY

Meet my family
  Off springs of the same paternity
  Sharing the same fraternity
  Knitted into one indivisible entity
  Bearing the same identity
  Beneficiaries of the same legacy
  Brought into the same community
  Forming an object of immense perplexity
  Displaying beauty in all diversity
  Issues of profound majesty

Meet My family
  They know my frailty
  They are aware of my deformity
  But choose to hype on my dignity
  They will rather loud my potentiality

As to encourage my productivity
Always forgiving my fatuity
But never condone my impunity
Though they protect my vulnerability
They insist on my accountability
To boost my sanctity

Meet my family
Declared guilty of the same offense
Victims of the same Adamic nature
Hopelessly awaiting the same verdict
Condemned to the same eternal death
But witnessed the same twist of judgment
Recipients of the same pardon
Purchased by the same priceless blood
Made holy by the same immutable Word
Adorned by the same redeeming grace
Fortified by the same unfeigned faith
Eagerly awaiting His glorious return[1]

---

1. Tribute to all the people I refer to as family

10

THE EPIPHANY

Trudging down the rough Emmaeus way
With hearts muddled with grief and dismay
The twosome began their lonely journey
Seeking answers to their questions
The trauma of last Friday still fresh on mind
Wasn't He brutally murdered the other day?
Wasn't His body in Joseph's custody?
What is this news about His missing body?
What now is this story about the empty grave ?

Discreetly, a third man joined
Wondering why the resurrection news
brought them such amount of sadness
"Are you only a stranger here?"
Cleopas retorted quite disturbed
Who doesn't know Jesus, our Christ?

who our leaders unjustly murdered!
Are you really unaware
Of Golgotha's gruesome murder?

"Aren't you fools?" the third Man quizzed
"Christ was meant to suffer these things"
According to the scriptures
When to their destination they finally reached
The third Man feigned more miles to cover
"Stay for the night"
the twosome urged
At the breaking of bread
their epiphany came
The lone man they met
on their lonely road
Was the risen Christ
they desperately sought

So when you trudge your rough Emmaeus way
Your heart muddled with grief and dismay
And you walk your lonely journey
Seeking answers to your questions
The trauma of last Friday still fresh on mind
Though hope may seem brutally murdered
Always urge the third Man to stay for the night
For at the breaking of bread,
your epiphany will come
Never you miss the lone Man
on your lonely road

For He is the risen Christ
you desperately sought

11

A MATE FINALLY FOUND

HE WAS THE FIRST human
   Housed in that vast garden
   Rich in all kinds of fruits
   The acidic and the succulent
   Habouring all kinds of animals
   The big and the small
   All to keep him company
   Till Adam lost faith in them all
   For even in them all
   None met his longings
   Whether in the day or at night
   His boredom did increase

Till the creator looked down below
from His dwelling place above
He found the man He made

Lost in the world he was to rule
Cringed only to his corner
drowned deep in his isolation
Loathing all his neighbors
searching just for a mate
Neighbors who bore the names he gave
But couldn't give the friendship he craved
So back to work once again
The Almighty creator found Himself

During a deep slumber
The first surgery did foster
To find a rib to make him a mate
The feeling was intense
The sensation was dense
When Adam first saw her
"You are the bone of my bone
And the flesh of my flesh!"
He exclaimed in satisfaction
The animals were there
The birds were there
The trees were there
When at last man found a mate.

12

THEY ARE CALLED ANGELS

THEY ARE CALLED ANGELS
God's special messengers
They never tire
They never stagger
Always in gear
From one end of the heaven
To the other end of the earth
Taking orders from the Creator
Delivering orders to the created

They are called Angels
Man's special aide-de-camp
Their mission is vast
Their responsibilities are great
Their actions are swift
Though we don't always see them

But we always feel them
In the peace that defy the rancor
In the near misses that defy the danger

They are called Angels
The bringers of our good news
I do not know all their names
But how can't I know Gabriel?
"You will be with a child!"
Gabriel said to Mary
Nine months later
The first carol was sung
Here lies the good news
That changed my world and yours

13

THE SAINTS I KNOW

I KNOW QUITE A number of them
  Maybe not their faces
  Maybe not their names
  But for sure, their works
  Certainly their labour
  From the petty and the uncelebrated gestures
  Like lighting the lamp on the altar
  In that remote village church
  To the colossal, heroic, herculean feats,
  Like journeying across the continents
  With the message of forgiveness
  The selflessness of those believers
  Is their signature inscribed on walls of my faith.

I know quite a number of them
  Maybe not their faces

Maybe not their names
But for sure their tribulations
Certainly their unimaginable perils
From the cruel mocking and scourging,
The stoning and slaying
All borne for the Lord they hold so dear
Like the early church during the reign of Nero
To the fierce and brutal repression
Of the church today in some countries
The spilt blood of those believers
Is their signature inscribed on the walls of my faith

I have seen quite a number of them
Maybe not their faces
Maybe not their names
But for sure their unprecedented gestures
Certainly their unbeatable sacrifices
From their humility and availability
Like the missionaries in unpleasant places,
Who are completely sold out for Christ
To the wonderful men and women
Who God sends my way daily
All these are the saints I know

14

DON'T CALL ME THAT

DON'T CALL ME A failure,
That's what I'll never be,
I may not have seen,
the plenteous harvest yet,
I may not have known,
the goodly lot yet,
The bountiful desired result,
May still seem far away
But time they say
The acid test of value,
And I can tell,
I am not a failure.

Failure is crippling but I soar,
Higher than the eagles,
Failure is dwarfing but I am tall,

Taller than the steeple,
And I can tell,
I am not a failure.

Don't call me frustrated,
That's what I will never be,
My countenance for sure,
A little mirth may have shown,
For the quality of labour,
Hasn't met same quality of harvest,
Though time they say,
The acid test of value,
But tarrying you know,
How frustrating can be,
Yet I can tell,
I am not frustrated.

Frustration is maddening but I am sane,
Saner than the psychiatrist,
Frustration is destabilizing but I am firm,
Firmer than the Everest,
And I can tell,
I am not frustrated.

15

In Times Like This

It was in times like this
   That Sisera the captain of the troops arose,
   Against the Israelites he mightily oppressed,
   Until in Israel Deborah arose,
   A mother and a prophetess embedded in one,
   And by her decree heaven was engaged,
   The stars in their courses the combat joined,
   Until God's people their liberty regained.

It was in times like this,
   That David and his young men in rage arose,
   Fast! they girded every man his sword,
   'Cause Nabal the fool their anger had torched,
   Until from Nabal's house Abigail arose,
   A wife and a negotiator embedded in one,
   'Quick!' her command resonated in the hills,

And just in time, her household was saved.

It was in times like this,
That Haman, the Agagite arose,
To annihilate all the Jews, not just a few,
Until from the palace Esther arose,
A queen and an intercessor embedded in one,
And by her wisdom Haman was cowed,
After the ripples the verdict was turned,
The Jews would live and Haman would die.

And in times like this,
Terrorism, war, and uncertainties have arisen,
Against humanity they mightily oppress,
From every part of the world prayers are raised ,
Believers and intercessors embedded in one,
And by their decrees heaven is engaged,
The stars in their courses the combat have joined,
And by His grace victory is assured.[1]

---

1. Dedicated to all intercessors.

16

Isn't It Weird?

Isn't it weird?

As babies we want to touch everything
As children we get excited over everything
As teens we want to explore everything
As youths we think we can conquer everything
As adults we want to control everything
But as the aged we lose taste in 'every' thing
For then we understand that real peace isn't in things
But only in beings

Isn't it weird?
In words we dream to love
But in act we love to dream
We yearn for love that is never there
But neglect the love that is ever there
We adore the people we may never meet

But ignore the neighbour we always meet
We donate our millions to faceless folks
But neglect the needy down the street

17

Papa's Old Hymn Book

The old red hymn book
    Lying silently on the floor
    Gazing helplessly all around
    Waiting for users that seldom come
    Because your owner is dead and gone

The old red hymn book
    Have your days of glory gone?
    Has your relevance dropped so low?
    You were afore time held so high
    And none but him could lay you hold

The old red hymn book
    Would you let me make you mine?
    Though your pages are parched and worn
    And your cover dry and torn

Yet you remain a symbol rare
Of my father's heart of love[1]

---

1. In the sweet memory of my father who went to be with the
Lord on the 12th day of September 2014.

18

OLD TRAVELLERS

THEY ALL LOOK WEARY
They look tired and used
Their once new shoes
Now filled with rips and holes
Once gorgeous attire
Now patched and faded
All point to the roughness of the road
The relics of time and tide

They all have different bags
No two bags are the same
Not in content nor in type
For no two individuals are the same
Not in content nor in type
So everyone hangs his bag

"Whence comest thou, oh travellers?
And whence goeth thou?"
"This journey started long before our birth
And will continue long after we're gone
The bags you see
Are the experiences we have
The patches on our attire
Are wrinkles from time and tide"

19

MY MEMORY

MANY EVENTS FILL THERE
    Some so bad, some so cruel
    And the very thought of them
    Make my heart shiver
    How did I live them?
    When loved ones wallowed in pain
    Fighting for their very lives
    Longing for healing that never came
    Till they breathed their very last

    All the times we spent together
    All the events we lived together
    All the dreams we shared together
    Outbursts of joys as well as of pains
    The ups as well as the downs
    All now relegated to one corner

My memory

Why can't I see them again?
Day break races to night fall
People move about their businesses
Conversations gone back to normal
No one seems to care about them anymore
'Cause they only exist in one place
My memory

There also existed
Moments so high and gay
Experiences so cool and good
With loved ones lost in ecstasy
Of dreams becoming reality
Of news too good to be true
How did I live them?
The nostalgia so raw and green
Wishing life would let me choose
I'd gladly relive them again
My memory

20

MY CHILDHOOD CHRISTMAS

YOU ARE HERE AGAIN
    The Christmas season
    My childhood was all about you
    The only time we'd visit our hometown
    Cousins big and small
    Aunties and uncles far and near
    Grandmas and grandpas
    All the people we held dear
    This's the only time we all unite

    Houses in twinkling bright
    Beautiful decorations of garlands
    Colorful lights and jingles
    Special family delicacies
    The late night gist and giggles

Capturing our little minds with rapture
But just as we thought it's just starting
Oops it's already over
We'd have to wait till another year

21

MYSTERY

MYSTERY

Isn't it what it's called?
Watch babies in the morning
Become men in the evening
They run around
They chuckle aloud
In the innocence
Of their infancy

They eat, they drink
They vex, they sulk
They play, they sleep
That's the routine
That's the rhythm
That's how it is,
That's how it's meant to be

That's how it should be

We watch them grow
They watch us wane
The bigger their picture
The smaller our image
The more they increase
The more we decrease
And soon we retire
While they refire
For such is life
Then the turn returns

The babies in their morning
Will be the men in their evening
They will watch them grow
As they will watch them wane
And soon they will retire
While their children will refire
Will there ever be an end?
When will it ever end?

Mystery
That's what we call it
The turns in life belongs to Him
"Will there ever be an end?
When will it ever end?"
Only Him can answer
For only Him is the Answer

22

MY DEAR SON

- -

MY DEAR SON,

    How I hate to see you this way
    Gazing unblinkingly into empty air
    Searching for hope everywhere
    Yearning for help in directions rare
    Seeking solution in all and sundry
    Asking questions, getting no reply
    Watching open doors shutting rudely
    Watching daylight dimming slowly

My dear son,
Why do you choose to travail this way?
Tongue parched as in desert land
Legs wearied as in unguarded journey
You stagger home every night
Weighing heavily on your unkempt bed

Sighing both in fatigue and despair
Wondering when and where
Your deepest hope will come

My dear son,
Why on earth did you choose such a path
That neither of us can walk you through?
What song is great except it be sung?
Which book is masterpiece except it be read?
The taste of the pudding isn't it in the eating?
Why choose this path where you know no tasters
Why tottering in a field void of singers
Why dwell in an area where you may find no readers

My dear son,
I have always wished you would let me into your mind
To access your thoughts and to massage your heart
To let you see that there's no failed hope with God.
My son, if it's God that gave you this song,
He will bring you singers
If it's Him that wrote you this book,
He is committed to sending you readers
And if He's the one that made this pudding,
Tasters will certainly abound

My dear son,
Would you do me a favor?
If it isn't God that
Made this pudding

Gave this song
Wrote this book
Would you let Him do
Whatever else He chooses?[1]

---

1. Dedicated to my dear son as he struggles through life and
   career.

23

HE HAS THE ANSWER

I LOOK AT THE face I have always known
Young and stark, and plain
Not backing out, not lagging
Energetic, feisty, unbending
Will you end a good song not sung?
A good book never read?
The weatherman can't tell
The newsman can't say
I wish I had the answer
I would have let it out before your calls
I wish I knew where to get it
I would have saved it for you
Only one Being has the answer

And in Him we put our trust.[1]

---

1. To my dear son as he struggles through life and career.

24

THE SOWER

The Sower, the Sower
  He carries his bowl
  It's filled with seeds
  He heads to his farm
  And casts them all there
  Then he heads back home

'The Sower the Sower
  What happened to your bowl?
  'T was filled with seeds
  Why now empty?
  Why plant those seeds
  When they could be eaten?'
  'The bowl is discarded
  For the fruits are multiplied
  The proceeds are now in barns

Because the harvest is here
To give bread to the eater
And more seeds to the Sower

25

My Church

Though our personalities differ
our resemblances transcend our differences
Our similarities outweigh our disparities
The origin of our bond date far in history
Reaching down to the pedigree we all share
Forming the intricacies of our filial tie
Issues of diverse tribes and tongues
Existing in multiple complexities
But united in faith of the risen Christ

Far from perfection we all are
From the pulpit to the pew we all err
None is perfect, not even one
For it's in the search of redemption
We found the cord that tied us all
The rock of our salvation

Sometimes we disagree and fight
When we let our emotions and not our hearts
Play the judge they know little about
Then soon we despair and desire
For the warmth we manufacture
When we share in fellowship together
For only in God's love we transpire
The true image of our Redeemer
Who gave His life for the Church

26

He's Working Behind The Scene

GIGGLING WITH LAUGHTER
It was a relaxed atmosphere
How on earth could that be?
When the wreckages of the damages
Lie littered everywhere
The signature of a damaged society
The symbol of a failed system
From whence then cometh laughter?
From same hearts wounded the most?

We then turned to ask why
We returned to get an explanation
Demanding why joy instead of depression
Why calm though bruised
And why count their blessings

In the midst of their losses?

And here's what they said:
"What is left outweighs what has left
What is left cannot be stolen
Our peace is far beyond the look
Our joy is dependent on the Rock
Our treasure is hidden far away
Away from where rot and moth live
So we know that come what may
He is working behind the scene."

27

COME TO OUR AID

THERE ARE TIMES I wish You would act faster
That You would arise and quench the dagger
Cutting through the fibers of our heart
With no regards to what we have to suffer
From the hurts their wounds fester
We struggle for what is ours
We beg for what belongs to us
Our enemies are stronger than us

We choke and cannot breathe
The giants have blocked our space
We gasp for air that's not there
Has our hope become a mirage?
The blizzard bites leave no respite
The avalanche of fear encompasses us

And none can save us but You
For our enemies are stronger than us

So what are you waiting for Lord,
When will all these end
How long do You have to look on
Till our enemies see our nakedness
Aren't You touched by our misery
By the pains from the cruel blows
The heartaches from the injustices?
Will there ever be a respite?

Widows have been denied of their rights
The poor have been trampled under feet
The people on high have ruled with impunity
No one regards their cry
Come quickly to our refuge oh Lord
Arise and deliver us from this flood
And rescue us from the impeding deluge
For no one else can help but You [1]

[1]Dedicated to the poor and the oppressed in the society

28

THE COMMUNION TABLE

MASTER, MY CHILD IS ailing
She needs your healing
Please make her whole

Woman, my bread's for my children
How can I offer my bread
To some hungry dogs?

Master, the crumbs are for dogs
Can I be the dog
The hungry dog
Under your table?

Woman, my body is the bread
The drink is my blood
Can I give my flesh and blood

To some hungry dogs?

Master make me Your own
Your very own
A partaker of Your table
The blessed communion

Woman your faith is enough
Come with your all
Come to my table
Where healing abound

29

ABOUT THE AUTHOR

Amara Ifeakor-Ezenwa is a prolific writer, poet, and a blogger. Her inspiring articles transcend different subjects. A marriage counsellor, life coach, and public speaker, she holds a Master's degree in Educational Psychology, Guidance and Counselling, and a Post-graduate diploma in Theology. Amara is passionate about Christ, and she pastors a church with her husband in Rennes, France, where they live with their two children. She works as a school facilitator.

30

OTHER BOOKS BY THE SAME AUTHOR

AMAZING DISCOVERIES – UNCOMMON treasures in the scriptures you need to know

Finding And Exploring My Divine Blueprint -Embarking on a life-changing journey of discovering my original pattern

Trouver Et Explorer Son Plan Divin – (French version of FINDING AND EXPLORING MY DIVINE BLUEPRINT)

Just Like A Hidden Treasure – Unveiling the tremendous insight in the parable of the
hidden treasure).

Just Like A Mustard Seed – (Unveiling the tremendous riches in the parable of the mustard seed)